P9-DFA-018

The Wireless Room

Shane Rhodes

NEWEST PRESS

© Copyright Shane Rhodes 2000

All rights reserved. The use of any part of this publication reproduced, transmitted in any form or by any means, electronic, mechanical, recording or otherwise, or stored in a retrieval system, without the prior consent of the publisher is an infringement of the copyright law. In the case of photocopying or other reprographic copying of the material, a licence must be obtained from the Canadian Reprography Collective before proceeding.

Canadian Cataloguing in Publication Data

Rhodes, Shane, 1973-
  The wireless room

  Poems.
  ISBN 1-896300-15-4

  I. Title.
PS8585.H568W57 2000   C811'.6   C00-910231-0
PR9199.3.R4642W57 2000

Editor for the Press: Douglas Barbour
Cover design: Duncan Campbell
Author photograph: Arion Predika
Cover photograph by Malak. J.P. Henderson in the Wireless Room, Dominion Observatory, 1949 reproduced with the permission of Malak. Copyright National Archives of Canada.

NeWest Press acknowledges the support of the Canada Council for the Arts for our publishing program. We also acknowledge the financial support of the Government of Canada through the Book Publishing Industry Development Program (BPIDP) for our publishing activities.

Some of these poems have appeared in: *Prairie Fire, The Fiddlehead*, CBC Radio's *Alberta Anthology, West Coast Line, Siglo* (Tasmania), and a chapbook entitled *Claims* published by filling Station press.

Sources: "its white and aimless signals " From Jack Spicer's "Thing Language" in *The Collected Books of Jack Spicer*, Santa Barbara: Black Sparrow Press, 1980, p. 217.
"short growing season is no explanation" From Adrienne Rich's "Sources" in *Your Native Land, Your Life*, New York: W. W. Norton & Company, Inc., 1986, p. 13.

Acknowledgements: There are many writers and friends who have helped this book, or the writer of this book, on its way. I would like to thank a fraction of them: Chris Wiseman, Ross Leckie, Sue Sinclair, David Seymour, Cybèle Creery, Rajinderpal S. Pal, Tonia Snell, Nancy Batty, Boyd Schwartz, the filling Station writing collective in Calgary, and the ice house writing collective in Fredericton.
  Thanks to my editor Douglas Barbour, and all the great people at NeWest, for their support, suggestions, and advice.
  Thanks also to my family for the stories they have given (and the ones I have taken).

NeWest Publishers Limited
Suite 201, 8540-109 Street
Edmonton, Alberta T6G 1E6
(780) 432-9427

1 2 3 4 5 04 03 02 01 00

PRINTED AND BOUND IN CANADA

25 Variations on a Dedication

for those who believe the spring an emmenagogue
for their brains bleed
for those who exhausted s from the dictionary
for those who have taken and lost women
in the papillary ridges of alberta
only to be haunted by the scent of wolf willow
for the man who stocked his head with trout
for sexual positions involving couscous
for those who have locked their super heroes in a freezer
as a test of their inherent strength
for any farmer who has purchased climax timothy
and blushed at the counter
for creeping red fescue
for crested wheat grass
for the man whose legs I compared to rivers
which made this city creak
for the peas killed by frost
for every chapatti that does not rise
for those who threw beer cans into the river
and refused to throw the plastic holder
for every mouth reminded of locker rooms
by the taste of parmesan
for those who believe polyglossia can compensate
for missing limbs
for those who approached a grizzly in a national park
not realizing that a grizzly like a poem
should not be approached without the proper rituals
for the proper rituals
for those who believe polyglossia can compensate
for the rent
for those who must repeat
for those who have never driven a hundred miles of gravel
for those who have never stained their hands with turmeric
for they have never tasted time

Contents

"In the imagination, instruments assembled—unseen cymbals just ajar that would collide with a resonance no more strident than a whisper; drums an inch below their padded sticks with palms ready to muffle them; oboes slanting, their reeds mute for a moment more; brass and woodwind waiting; fingers stretched motionless across the wires of a harp and fifty invisible bows poised in the air above fifty invisible sets of strings."

Patrick Leigh Fermor, *A Time of Gifts*

"You can't always dance to fiction."

Cornershop, *Womans Gotta Have It*

Home Roads

How easy these gravel roads seem
as if laid out in pre-history. The night air
full of wings: meadowlarks, dragonflies and overhead
a jet splits the sky, a scalpel in a Caesarean.
In the distance, a pick-up truck fades away
with the oiled ease of the mechanized,
a planned thing dragging dust clouds,
its tail-lit fire soon snuffed out by dark.
Walking from the car, each step is one across oceans
into foreign countries.

The Larkins' slough tonight
tunes up for an acoustic event, mosquitoes
search the air for blood-soaked chords
and the fence, a four-stringed instrument of silence,
sounds the sound of between. As kids, we thought
fences were here to keep us in,
but now "No Trespassing" signs dot the road
in stalled conversations.

And how many hours or years have I driven
to escape the city, only now to sense its magnetism
radiating through the air like musk?
The distant glow of street-lights
smog the horizon.

Grain is taken to elevators, cattle
to market and kids to college:
slaughterhouse rules,
once gone, you are not supposed to return.

The meadowlarks think I've come to see them tonight
and, anxious divas, break their throats in song. And maybe I have
or maybe I don't know why my memory takes over out here
so I walk through two worlds, haunting the place I grew up
and being haunted by it, a ghost without allegiance
in houses possessed by the living.

Or maybe I keep this place in mind
for I feel its homecoming will cleanse me:
the tractor dozing beyond that ridge
of poplar trees, the abandoned barn falling
into memory, writing another, quieter, history—
one that is momentary yet absolute.

Or is this where some part of you lives
the lives your parents understood
where the landmarks are known
by who broke ground and was broken by it?

The sun barely down. Deer test shadows
and wade into grass.

                    We live on
or move on, coming back only to stare
with eyes of immigrant wonder:

this slow, summer-long,
coming into seed.

Whippoorwill
(*caprimulgus vociferus*)

This is memory's memory of forgetting
a thought that exists only as sound at the
edge of a sky a noise you turn to
expecting nothing for it's made of
nothing but your turning and a sound
more silent than a black and white
and these are the thoughts
making the sun go down as the
last visible itch is gathered
between their wings, goat suckers,
mosquito eaters, whales of the sky,
endings start in their call—more
night than morning, more sunset
than day—they show us to our seats
put the film in backwards
and leave us in the trailer.

Twilight, Watervalley Hills

These hills roll, slurred and long,
a drunk's conversation at a family reunion.
Here where horizons are made and laid at the edge of feet
and the drunk moans on, sculpting his actions into legend
—holding a niece's breast to his ear
listening for the sea,
reciting Reader's Digest anecdotes
to an empty Buick in a parking lot,
burping unrecorded Mahler symphonies—
legends that will be told and retold
so the family machine grinds on
to the sound of his snoring.
Roads are pressed by tires
of campers, motorhomes, tent trailers, people
hurrying back to the city,
tired with their work,
worn by their leisure.
And the drunk rambles on, oblivious
to the shadows that stain him,
his talk works its way into his sleep
and ours and the hills
bend from our view into night's cool water
lungs full of mosquitoes, black flies and intoxicant air.
And the family wonders why it structures love and loathing
in such official ways, what process of evolution
directs us back to our own and away again
in unending cycles of attraction and repulsion.
And they dream of planets
bending in and out of the shadows.
And they dream of a train that crosses their night
digesting distance.

And somewhere the perfect families breathe easy
and sexless in their archived sleeps
as the drunk staggers and falls
beneath the volleyball net,
his head against the dirt, listening
to the earthworms fucking,
to the shed wings of medieval beasts,
to the quiet, cooling voltage of his blood.
His son brings him a blanket and hides his nakedness
among the croquet bats and sand pails.
Last last light illuminates the mountains,
boozy and furled in the distance—
they mix and merge
with the white-topped clouds
as if only now forming memory.

Haynes Town Store

my grandmother and father said
to my father said
to me said

—if you sat here long enough
you could count the population in an hour
using one eye and two hands and
if you sat here long enough you could
do the post-mortem best to start at the curling rink
and move on to the outdoor skating rink and the
catholic church all disguised as the heart but the store
and the layers of tobacco spit on the floor and while
well I don't know for sure but somebody
must have 'whittled' here once if you sat here long enough
then must have been here even before the first train
hit the last cree crossing the main street and the
last mastodon lost itself between the coke machine and
the erratic chevy the other side of the pleistoscene
if you sat here long enough, the store was there
before, I'm sure—

                                        my grandmother said

—he comes from the southeast coast of china as a boy
(or a man or as far as I can figure out
wing wong was a hundred all his life)
and after two months on ship or so it is said
in vancouver he buys a pound of chocolate
and after two months of rice and salt water
it tasted of tears   wing speaks no english yet
has selling in his blood like the last dime in his pocket
he buys more chocolate and breaks it into ten pieces
and sells each piece to the immigrants off the boats
for 5¢ each to people like wing or you or me hungry for land
or anything that looked like dirt and tasted like the dust storm
wing bought his store with
and a bag full of nickels—

                                              but, I said

—why would he settle here
in this spurline clot of grain dust and
sedimentary white puritanism there must be a billion
such towns joined together by clay silica rail
and conjunctions like some nervous system waiting
for wing to look out the train window at the red deer
river valley and say he saw a city in twenty years
the land he would buy for pennies and sell for thousands and
what else wing you crazy chinaman they asked *what else do you see*
wing wong says a store and they laugh as he touches the map
with a piece of chocolate and grinning says *here*
the store will be here—

—during the war or so it is said (but it's all
said, every last bit) wing and another store owner
each bought a box car of sugar believing war rations
would raise prices and profit accrue like
bullets in europe but with war came price control
and so wing said looking over his car full of sugar
where's the money now there it is
a classical problem and wing dreams blizzards
of sugar, blood sugar, everything a bit too sweet
while the other guy, sugary white, sells sells sells
popularity wing thought in his sleep must be bought
so he lowered his prices below cost
and packed sugar by night and sold it by day
his skin dusted white as people from as far as red deer
come to buy the crazy chinaman's sugar
("How much for that bag? You're kidding? We'll take ten!")
he'll be ruined thought the other store owner
as he packed by day and left by night
and wing almost ruined himself he said later
before the other guy fled and wing made them pay—

but look, I said

—a tour

and the store we haven't even seen the store yet and there's
a reason for that there's not much there most would say
it's a bloody eyesore imagine a house above a garage to the
side broken fuel pumps leaning against the almost broken
fuel pumps everything limping up to the hollow edge of
uselessness ascending to antique and then the old-time carriage
stalls filled with petrified horse shit of long-ago-made-into-glue
($1.10 a bottle, beside the chainsaws) clydesdales and arabians and
what ever the hell breed fifty-horse snowmobiles with all too
uncertain half lives and the two-hundred-horse wasp-nest slash
tractor slash rustmine off in the corner cultivating its own peculiar
entropy it takes a mad species of order just to find the door an
irrational sort of patience just to comb through the conflicting
curves of space and two-by-fours and fenders and the manic
manifest mind of quack-grass popping up through the pavement
just to figure out why the kerosene is beside the twinkies and who
mixed the bullets with the fruit and what put the motor oil in the cooler
one needs half a mind just to keep the other half from losing the
nervous thread of logic placing the train tracks not even a block away
(but it's all "not even a block away") running like an epileptic
corpus callosum through the middle of town, of the hamlet, of the
to-be-or-not-to-be if somebody had the strength to ask the question
who would be left to answer one can't be sure but must
have the heart of giants or the time the time the time of fossils
to sit here, and let it all work out—

17

                                    my grandfather (ralph) said

—if you sat here long enough
you could see the continent shift
between the tracks of wing's new studebaker
picking feldspar on his land across from us
granitites piled high on the leather back seat
why wing my grandfather asked
why not use my goddamned pickup
ralph wing said his body striated keeping time
and I want him to say something like *palaeogene*   or
each man must pick his rhyolites how he can   or
mind your own damned business ralph   but no
wing says *ralph because I can't I'm an old man*
ralph I can't lift the rocks (evaporites) that high
and my grandfather laughs claps wing on the back
across the fence silt sifts from their shirts
in the back seat of wing's new studebaker
a continent shifts, if you sat here long enough—

One Whole Year Wasted

They came from the old country,
my grandmother tells this and insists on calling it
the old country. In her mind, she travels with them.

At the american immigration office, a man tells them,
To live here, you must learn english. Out with the old.
German for english—in this country, it's all a fair trade.
Grandmother tells this looking at her hands.

So they work on a farm for one year, for it is all they know.
Every day a new word melts into their tongues
like a pad of butter. They are glad to be understood
and scold each other when they lapse into german.
Within a year, their muscles are hard with a working knowledge
and they go back to the immigration office
and tell the man (the same man?) we know english
are ready to become americans.
The puzzled look on the man's face surprises them
as he scurries off and leaves them talking english proudly,
german all but a faint sour odour.

(She's told me this story four times
each time it changes.)

The immigration man brings in another man
and asks the couple to speak.
The man is puzzled, as is the other.

Does anybody in this country speak english? the couple asks.
Finally a man comes who is not puzzled
and speaks english back to them.
They are proud and say the words they had heard so often
between the farmer and his wife.
The office men grin. My great-grandparents grin.
Everyone seems happy.

Except—this is the point grandmother's been getting to—
Except, the man tells them, you aren't speaking english at all!

What! they say in english are you nuts?
How long have you lived here? Don't you know this
is english? they say in english. He looks
around the office nervously. No,
it isn't, he insists in norwegian.

My grandmother laughs and continues in english.
One whole year wasted, and the callouses,
not english but norwegian. My grandmother
chuckles, looks at her hands, and continues in english

a moving poem
for Cybèle

What will drive us apart
now drives us together—
this dotted lane on which
we've signed for a week
leaving all that's left
to leave:

> Calgary, some rubbers
> in a hotel parking lot,
> a shaving kit in Winnipeg, a shoe
> in Montreal—our lost
> luggage a continental
> connect the dot.

Our time is this car
pushed through a parking lot.
The heart's a fan for the radiator.
The hand hugs the wheel hugs the road
hugs like a lover's departure. All for this
cost for a coast to the coast, for this
stalled good-bye, while we smile
for that commercial that will be
shot featuring the dead
forests of our passing.

I kiss your glove and whisper:

"I'm taking the keys
with me, love."

looking back to looking back to gommorah

for once you could say we were part of a
great and sexy art, yes, rehearsed our lines
thoroughly, you standing by the frigid
aire with a smile and me, well, what was I
doing? staring at the crotch of the man
ikin no doubt, working on the fine points
of rhythm, watching the lights from downtown
hamburg in the overcast, o the lines
my dear we had the spring and then thank god
a break and we chatted between the tab
le and the couch, wiped our lips again no
doubt you touched your nose to your sleeve and we
shivered to your thought, all the improper
ly weighted lines, but we rehearsed, we re
hearsed the lines thoroughly then we turned to
the city your face reflected in the
window, someone set a cup on the pi
ano and stumbled into the keys (the
sound a roused grey dust), and remarked, "those eyes
the sweat on your thighs" and I, surprised by
the feeling of such . . . How your hair fell so
precise and slow, so slow and still, your waist
caught on the window sill, yet the vase and
the last of the stumbled notes

A Painted Screen

You laughed the way someone in a sinking ship or a falling plane laughs or how someone, before a battle, breaks out in hysterics. It's what the mind is left with when words have nothing to say, when our sentences only cover so much of us. The moon, even if you could see it, was nowhere to be seen. I remember gladiolus in a clear glass bowl half filled with water as once being an integral part of summer. But now, in this place of elms and poplars, summer carries a hole in it, a place for gladiolus in a clear glass bowl half filled with water. Telling me your story—after we had made love on your small bed, through the summer heat—you laughed and your laughter left a hole in me, fiercely articulate. I touched your shoulders with my hands and was filled with a furious wonder. But there are times when thought shuts down and we walk in strange corridors of ourselves like hotels we have never seen and we open each door we come to and with great detail note the mahogany counters, the yellow shag carpet, the plastic-wrapped cups beside the sanitized sink and it is only the details we can come back with and not what they mean. The distance is illusion, a painted screen the water of thought crashes beside. You said when you told them, they disowned you as if you were the dangerous one and that's when he came at you with a knife. But, after the first time, you sat by the window staring at the horizon of the prairie through the poplar trees covered with their own green flame. The tops of the leaves tinged with orange and yellow as your grandfather's semen leaked out of you onto the warm cushions of the couch. And you said there was a kind of peace there almost unnameable and unconnected to what had just happened and would happen again before the month was through, the second time even more forced, more blood, more violent. And there are times when we must just state the story and leave it, for, if we do not, it will loop us back into the unending language that protects an event. And it will overtake us and eat our being. And our caution will fall like night through the wheat. You sat and watched the sunset through the trees and I imagine, touching your shoulders in this summer heat in this room, that room and your skin and the light as it played in the moment of the thickness of glass and somewhere the smell of gladiolus and the glistening clearness of first twilight as it trapped in the drops of cum that dried at your knees.

Clytaemnestra

The points of view are unanimous,
agreeing to the gears of the event
down to the unbickerable exactitudes.
Except her hair with the air of mountain meadows.
We missed that. Staring off to the distance
and the laundry drying in the wind like kites.
Deposits of pure and invisible blue reason.
The passing boats filled instantly
with rumour that buttons had been thrown off.
Burst, really. Onto the table and into the sea.
There to accumulate shells, starfish, aquamarine culture.
Our great reckonings taken by all for cause for wonder.
What are curves, it is agreed, that are quicker than these.
Their concise loungers filled with bouquets of possibility
before the current tossed them ashore. The words
pass between her mouth and mine, in a bed that smelled
of others, the machinery of her face munching
the tithe of my affection. X. Y. They are here too,
saying, "Avenge her desertion (mountains!
air!). Mute the last flight of stairs,
the pigeon's iridescent wings in the court,
the mahogany chair she will toss with her anger, do it all
so her leaving will leave the drama to the houseflies.
Murder would do in a pinch, the art of the moment
so intense and counselling one could dispense
with the justifications and get on with the work
we've been dying to do." Fortified by the reasons
since I got up, spitting grape seeds out the window
onto the passers-by below, I touched your naked shoulder
and said, "So we can get on, now. The sash is stirring.
A slight inshore breeze. Coffee on the wind and buttons I hear.

Stirred, I believe, by the wings of description. Wooden oars
on water. Between the spaces, there is motion. A flicker."

Each mealy thing and its described consistency, lying there,
one wonders in which attire do you address your needs?
But already there are problems. The surplus details
unmarketable, unremarkable, in general, divine.
The vision so strong, any bit will do. My sex,
if I had not said so much already. The embarrassments,
especially the male ones, spilled onto the floor,
rippling in particle-waves to the future there to be held
as relics of dust. Into accuracy and out again, like
darning needles, but also into its shadow,
there to knit the true music. Every salient push
negating another. The shore laid out like linen, white with salt.
There's nobody there. A homecoming worse than nothing.
It's big and grand, structured for loss, yet who really cares?
If only someone would say, scratching their behind,
"My longing sleeps at my hips, I have awayed so long"
or "I smell roses heavy with blood, and it is our blood"
or "The ocean, *its white and aimless signals . . .*"
that part would be easy. The wind beset
by grace as we get close to the atom
("mountains," "air"), the words like grains of tongue.
But something else happened and its explication does not
answer easily. As one who hears boats crashing
to shore and feels a grand deadening as he thinks it.
Like the mammal of the moment had eluded him
and snickers from the trees.
The diaphanous light, he would say, is not estimation,
but the flurry of life explained. Her skin, nailed down: here

and there. The sound and all its swallows. Her personality grows
in little drafts, bits of white space pasted to the air,
urging the fingers forward to what the nostrils tell us
is her sex but the eyes say sea, mountains, infinite time versus
eternal. As those who opened the gates
and pulled in the horse, thinking: wood, replica,
ornamentation, a great willingness to forget the past
under the monstrosity of a longed for closure.
The troops feeling satisfied, that they had for once
contained and sated an unfathomable hunger.
But—as light arrives—imbalanced
by a swimming darkness, their blood leaped out
like leaves. An unregulated space
yet one which regulates all others. Gloves on and blankets.
Half of which. A diver swimming into the sea.
Flowers, mountaintops, vegetative anomalies,
anemone-shaped things, all as the eye would actually see it.
Perturbed? Not in the least. But the air filled
with a melancholic sadness as between the thing
and rumour of its arrival. Who could have prepared for such
catastrophes, such losses? The sash is stirring and the sea. Footsteps
in the courtyard. Perhaps a little less and a little more
in the right places. Shock. Surprise. A stiffness in the knees.
Mountains. None to speak of except for the rift of furrowed skin
between her shoulders where her body formed
our expectations of rift, music, valley, morning air.
One could shower in the speculations. Were there? Here?
A roaring voice, hoarse with salted longing. Tell us
in a sentence what the stars have strived
ten years to create! Cup her warm breast
like a conch shell to your ear! Is it all action, product,

atomic-mass, encyclopedic visits to the pawnbroker?
What of his hair—ruffled in the wind of return? What of the rocks
and lichen? What of her body, waking, still bruised by sleep?
Suppose we have forgotten these too. Then what?
Roundly? Thrasonicle? Minstrel? Pause?

Ambassadors

When you hold your mother in your arms an
gels if there ever were any batter
their wings on street lights the snow melts the grass
dies and somewhere a stranger takes a child
's hand as your mother cries in the slow ferm
ata of a disease that first took her
youngest brother now turns its slow machine
ry to her and it's not something like grief
or look out the window and see a kest
rel and your own reflection in the sol
id pane as you let her go and you are
again the son who says ineffectual
things like Calgary or ineffectual
and you offer her in your own son hands
another bludgeon of flowers because
you bring the hammer down because what else
can you do in the hospital that gath
ers death up like a bouquet screaming quiet
quiet blues and this woman lets your hand
go as tears roll off her like stones why will
she age another year in a month why
the face you could so make love to you wish
you could just hold the hand she's dropped for one
second without seconds and hands shaking
and stops spinning

As Dusk Breaks Over Us

Lilacs unbloomed, like a kind of promise
through the middle of winter, a time,
however merciful, vengeful or indifferent,
chiselled into the snow-bound paths
of our warm-wanting. And I remember
this time of year the look in my father's face
whenever he killed something. It was
a step beyond love, so sure and deep.
To have adopted the wreckage, married it,
as a part of style, the turning mobile formed
and deformed by that which would erase it
from the air I breathe. The apartment walls,
their dramaturgy sizzling into the dream which is,
right now, this instant, tearing us in two.
The air so charged with paths, any moment
would not be the wrong one. Of our midland—
scarves flickering behind our necks—tour,
admittedly much has been forgotten
and we will need much recalling
if we are to get out of this season: blue plum,
saskatoon, high-bush cranberry, chokecherry, wild grapes.
Their names wound the tongue. We hardly remember
how or where the heat fits together with this flesh.
Was it June or July or vice versa?
And in my mind, the pornographic stir of waves.
Flocks of yellow birds displace the sky
with straw-colour wings rising from oil-soaked reeds.
We would sit there, on the edge of his bidding,

his hair like gilded air. The sky captured
in the distant water, where it plays along the crests
of waves, fenced and tamed. And we forget
the natural pain that makes us. How I think I
only knew my father when he was hurting,
or being hurt. I picture him in the doorway,
the light from the hall streaming around him,
his arms raised to the air in violation
or fear, it was so hard to tell which.
The gap between promise and pronouncement—
where the fishes swim. But the night will not
stop for the hotdog stands, and the local rowdy bars,
passing like a rolling pin over leavened dough
where our prayers are fixed between mouth
and suspected ear. But no, not that,
not in the least, haven't you been listening either?
The season has precluded it, abandoned to excess,
nothing more, and we have chased it down.
From the poem, a woman reaches toward us
from her dishevelled bed, her skin wrapped
in meridians, tropics, climata. She reaches
but her arms are warped by the optics of that place
or by the tears brimming in her eyes or ours, and we
cannot tell if she, like a pendulum in mid-swing, is
attracted or repelled, coming or going. I can
only do so much. We can only do so much.
Perhaps her mother is mad or her lover calling?
She waits for us but will not speak. Apogee. Another layer

to which we thought, ages ago, the last. Pisces.
Aries. There are moments when we edge toward
dissolution and nothing we know will drag us back.
No, snow ice-glazed. No, the ice itself like porcelain
freshly baked. The gods, "tossing them off like underwear,"
promise nothing. But perhaps a memory from a distance,
curving the present back into the past and so
our orbits go undiminished. Days pile up at the door.
You remember for no reason your father's face.
The light, when it comes, will arrive, will
falter, will drop to our feet in a motion
it has neither wanted nor longed for.

2

Claims

for N. Van Eaton

My father is dead
only a black and white picture
I always resented that
always resented my mother for that
marrying a black and white picture

He died that night February 26, 1974
a drink in his hand.
He drank himself to that spot for 20 years
but he was a good drinker   one of the best.

When they unhooked the hospital cords
tied the death tag on his toe with a slip knot
they thought he was through.
He tapped the doctor on the shoulder:

I'm thirsty he explained
need something to take with me
a wineskin a drink a strong whiskey.
But the doctor told him he was dead
and the dead shouldn't drink.

Spited.
My father swallowed the 30 years before him
and everything after

in one big drink.
He was thirsty

when he died

I remembered outside of Red Deer
my mother driving
my brother in the front seat.

(She cried   but no   that may be wrong   may not be true
she may not have cried)

I remember she said   *there*   pointing down
that's your father   pointing down   *that's him*
but who did she say it to
no   I can't remember
I was looking at my brother   wondering
wondering what our mother was doing
there   in a cemetery
  making up fathers

It happened once at the Empress in Rocky
I saw him there
off in a corner barely visible
behind the pool tables
and grey cigarette smoke.
The smoke made me positive
my father was not a smoker
so I knew it was him
my father   making things up.
That meant he was real.

But when I went to talk to him
talk to the father I hadn't seen in 20 years
he wasn't there
his tea coloured whiskey down to the first ice cube
fifty bucks beneath the glass.

That was it   gone again
not even a picture this time

I stopped him in the Empress hotel doorway
the wind blew in around us
hanging onto my father.
He said I could ask him one thing
one thing only.
So I asked the date of his birth
because, for some reason,
I still didn't know.
He said that was fair
and opened his mouth to tell me
but all that came out
was snow

claiming a familiar landscape

These are my father's boots
dried twenty years in dust
discovered like the body
of some family pet.
This mud between the grips
his only claim
on the landscape.

This is the truck he drove
left at an abandoned farm
with the unwanted junk.
See the beehive beneath the hood
the whiskey bottles in the back.
Slip your fingers over
the worn hand marks on the wheel.

This crystal glass I hold in my hand
(feel the rounded corners in your hand)
he fell into when he died.
Could you see a man
drowning in that?

This is a picture of him
drinking with friends
the prairie behind them   my father.
Some look at this picture
and smell salt water
from a drowned man's lungs.
Others point out   a resemblance.

And this is my father's boat
its hull still sharp smooth and lacquered black.
This is where I sit waiting
for the submerged life
of a dead man

Taken by a Kodak Brownie
no focus no batteries no bait.
You're unexpected as if you heard
the click and slowly turned to
your right eye blinks   the noise
lips moving.

Framed in the tall grey grass
on the grey hill behind the grey house
your hair catching the afternoon sun and almost almost
on the edge of colour.
Put that damn camera away,
your lips hint at an old conversation click
but I can't read between these shades of grey.

What a trick.
What a goddamned trick.

I look at this and think click
another second from your 34 years drops on the table
click like you never stopped living click
in these pictures of the dead.

I put the photo down my eyes sore
trying to think perspective build that other dimension
make the connection some hint of the word.

What's he saying Who's he looking at
What's missing Who's not here?

At the Empress
I sat with my father

and we talked like old friends.
When he finished his drink

he ordered two more
and we drank to new beginnings.

I didn't realize till after the first swallow
our drinks weren't whiskey at all

but salt water

My father winked

Colour is the first thing taken from you
your face set in chemicals and framed
by this white border like a grave
What a goddamned trick.

your body
sacrificed to the sun and the Kodak
your arms fade into your chest sinks into
your face they say the eyes are the last
to go eaten away by a sepia storm

only five months on the prairie
'til they till you under

I know now I shouldn't have brought you out
should have left you in the album pages
kept the hidden hidden the secret secret should have
stopped these questions should have
stopped

and forget about you for twenty years
that's development

light will leave no part of you
untouched but fade you to a blurry puddle of grey
and I will point to your picture to my children to theirs
Imagine

this is remembering

Claim

I think my father a grey god
who thought his thirst a muscle he could flex
and relax at will   he was a drop-out
alchemist changing wine to blood
the magician who one by one sawed
his family in two   the carpenter who brought
his house down   a drunk who couldn't
screw   I think my father was
the line   a k-mart chalice leaking
rum   he was a knife plotting
through an etherized family   who drew tears
from the crowd like a stomach pump   the man
who drank and puked two months in the basement
then stumbled up to ask where everyone
was   he was the sound of clapping
in an empty room   I think my father
wandered blind for weeks from his still-
made vodka and had his children wear
distinct colognes so he'd smell them apart
who outlawed bathing for a month while the tub
was full of gin   I think my father
a boat pounding through a storm
of reason   who died snorting the grammar
of a new sentence   I think my father
demanded we recite five generations
of lineage before we could enter the house
I think my father was

3

Meditation on the Electron

> "The electron wave is not a picture of an elec-
> tron, but only a visual representation of the
> chances of finding it somewhere in space."
>
> Robert Jones, *Physics as Metaphor*

öomph   ffhooh   sshoooh   Heft,
gatherlings. Lift, current spuds.
Ride the up draft valencies,
volt vultures. Up there,
engine heads. Circle, 1/2 spins,
schizophrenic Heisenburgians, heavers
heaving decimal points like shot-
put. Commas of the dark, God's
pause, whose claw of precision is
death. But rise, muscle mouths. Rise,
particle/wave, piston-fisted -ingers. Rise,

pole-positioned battery-punks with your
plug-in genitals. Ravenous couplers.
As the violin wears a G-stringed
phantom ear, vulva thick, you dance on
the head of a pin. Jolt jocks, chargers,
amberlings, I love the way you heat
physics' boil. I give you (double-lifed
circuit shocks) the lightning bolt (ubiquitous
negatrons) awakening, unstoppable images
of your chance.

Meditation on the Proton

If, like me, you desire to lose
yourself in things and believe you could
get in the canoe and truly push-
off, then let this be your star guiding

you across dangerous water. There are
places so crushed by gravity
that light collapses and
falls, perhaps,
into our lives. There, like a bat
trapped in a midnight house, we wish to
account it with our order and so contain the
unplaceable expanse within our own black wings. Finis. *The end*
they will tell us. *Put your junk*
in the garbage on the way out.

But for those
who have seen
the day slow down

and open new shops
of light?

Or have smelt the air of a man
fresh from cutting hay
who has bathed in our room?

What rituals of knowledge
will comfort us when even
language refuses to serve
precise and all the mind's
matched socks stammer and are
lost?

Come back to these bits, these
stitches of substance, always
there, always the chemist's children, always
first, always the last dance
is yours. They will take us
peacefully and without care
because time loves them and therefore
us, because only the object loved
has its teeth in proximity to the heart.
And look now, how far we have moved /

across it.

Meditation on the Neutron

like the rainbow
trout that fought its
way into our
hands only to
leave us the
hook of its name,

Meditation on the Tachyon

Nostalgia's particle,
a regret so tough even time
couldn't chew it
                    ptuie!   Light's
delinquents, demoted to déjà vu's spittoon
and the second-hand line of the continuous past
—the used car-lots of history.

Our yesterday is their tomorrow
our retro their new-age.
For the tachyon, science slowly uninvents itself,
peeling its proofs from the page
just as trees cram back into seed
and indoor plumbing creeps
back outdoors.

Word is,
they can't wait for Shakespeare
to erase all his plays.
                    In a way,
they evoke a certain Darwinian pity
for the dumb progress
of the devolved.

Their deaths, as big as wombs,
bawl with newness.

          (les maisons

de souvenir)

The invisible strings
which suspend disbelief,
pin-ups of the abstract,
they play for illogic's home-team.
But for all my fancy imaginations
they are eyeless bits of nothing,
moth wings, grey matter, unknowables,
made entirely of metaphors
with fins
—too fast for light.

Meditation on the Photon

We have stumbled into the anthology
of longing where our sad mass contemplates
reflections of itself in the smooth
sibilance of light. *Impossible*
the mirror whispers *impossible.* There are problems
with being this big yet thinking
this small.
But, like the pain you talked about
last night, curled up in the
corner of our thought, we have
bungled a universe
into a single word, hoping it
the eulogy of all we mean:
light.

In time, our image, like a bubble
rising from the creek bottom,
will be all that is left of us;
we will become pure and *quanta*, bundled
in time where our image is
currency, coined and at one
remove from the work of being—
the body's apocrypha and slang:
light.

But look,

> light is
> > the language
> > > between 'things'   mind

> > > > the gap, and push
> > > > into the dark you
> > > > so wish to know

Meditation on the Neutrino

Even silence has a life
and a monologue. Listen.

A woman in the apartment above yells *baby*
while a man on the street yells *screwdriver*.

Your body a blur, a particle
        of expectation,
                what the autumn light
              spiroid and derelict
finds beneath the sheets. Beneath
        my idea of it.
              But to swim through your flesh
     and see
           what has been left
and what has been taken:
              the closed-down reactor across the bay
                one red shotgun shell in the kelp
              crab bodies like unstrung violins
on the Bay of Fundy.
        With the waves crashing in.

                    Something
      on the verge of nothing—
               ravelling and un-
ravelling. Something
        on the verge
           of something.

The rain, which is mere word,
wets our hands.

Meditation on the Quark

To go in, as one would in ancient times,
with libations and the pouring out of grief.
To go in, though words
describe the action indifferently,
like the writing of pleasure.
There is something to be said for
there is always something to be said.
To go in, for our bodies crowd us
with meaning. The sound
is long and not wholly audible.
Spots of grass warmed by sun.
White houses in the heat,
shimmering. There is sadness
in everything we touch
not because it has fallen off
from a world undivided
but because there is a hole
your body fills, completely.
To go, then, in blindness, in mourning.
Did you think the heart would understand?
Poor heart. It was made for generalities
while the particulars kill us:
the way your lovers' mouths devours bread
how his hands are scored with work
how the imagination loves in parts
yet the body can only love the whole.
It's not all beauty and fucking Keats
off in the 19th century
coughing his lungs out. To go, then,
in fleeting motions.
Notice here the stalled
details, the peculiarities of chance.

On one side, we are leaving;
on the other, we have just arrived.
The trick is what is conveyed
is what is conveying. Motion
become substance. Much
will come of nothing.

Meditation on the Atom

We are always reinventing Troy.

Ten Seconds of Silence

On hearing the time signal—
all clocks applaud.

        Yet, if we turn our ear from it
will we stay forever young and
curfewless? Or, once caught
in the minute of inertia, (in the
scythe of its pendulum swing)
are we among the numbered
ambassadors, a broadcast

flock of metronomes? Time
wearing us?
And we must wonder, we
who hear it, will we still
rise into tomorrow, ethereal
and charged, ready for the encore
the way we did today, the way
all performers should: as beautiful
as we mean, as we mean to mean, as
we mean to be. Feathered
by the possible. And could
Champlain have been so wrong,
in Quebec, in 1608, mounting
his sundial next to his flag
proving only what is evident, that
time claims us its nation? The anthem
is our elegy, and a clock,
even one carrying the most
terrible hours in it, will never
wring its hands and
grieve.
But listen now, how the landscape of noon
lies untracked before us:
now, (in this cesium
instant)

We will age, it says,
as untouched strings.

Gravitas

Syntax of pull, strained
muscle guiding me down the
lines of your ribs, your
outcrop of hips. You
could well be the roust of a
much kinder geology.

Admit it, only a stoic would
think of apples. I
promise to let it all
fall for

        gravity's

              steady suck.

Newton said this,
        of course, is what math
             is for, to grasp
how the bed
        wants us
            to lie
in its pool
        of potential.

What we have learned thus far:
                Eros is geometric
                extended field theory

           We are preserved with salt,
           vinegar and a sense of loss

If you know a shorter way home,
take it

Loneliness is dark-matter
and only birds have hollow bones

The more you weigh—the more
it will love you

Go ahead, just try and
drop me

4

Tenderloin and Telephones

A)

I want to show you
this scar from my nipple to my
hip, received one night
from a man wearing a Timex
I could tell you, from the digital clock
glowing at the bedside, it happened
around midnight and, yes,
he too had impeccable
timing

You complain already
of greying hair, wrinkles,
indistinguishable aches

I want to tell you not
man, you're only 24,
which you are, but this at least
we will have in common, the new
lines drawn every day from the cooling
geometry of our bodies

And that our failings
in time will bind us

Your hand on my wrist
timeless as a watch

I want to tell you
events in the middle-ages were
timed to the pulse,
so something could happen
in a heart beat

a four-chambered
tick of blood

in the moment your
hand brushed mine and
moved off

B)

(all I need now is a sexier phone)
for t.

—and I wanted to say   love   I
could smell your breath of
tenderloin and wine   steamed
mussels and greens   taste
the fat on your lips
greasing my ear's throat—

—and I wanted to say   the
sound of the receiver
dragged over your contours of body
that it was like
         my hand was there
thick with listening

—and I wanted to say   I
thought nothing of the
alchemy of presence
unwiring distance

         or this
another night alone

listen

               last night

                    I wanted to say—

C)

(*le chat*)

for Sue & Dave

Your cat is violence
domesticus, with pelt and claws

Night long he humps
the cool grass on Charlotte Street

Breeds composure,
dreams sardine

His presence is killing
satire of your every thought

Voice, the sound
of locked-up brakes

But he tempts you,
with his lottery of purr

The mine
of his affection. Infinitely french, he

Bleeds
shadow

Curls-up on your pillow
like a fist

Sleeps all day
like a wound

D)

(for a present unreceived)

Someone in this town
has received my gift
    a lopsided sweater
knit all winter by you

    and it wasn't me

Canada Post fed this infidelity
with its queer logic of 'deliver,'
even the Queen sanctioned it
with ten 45¢ nods
of her many royal heads

    Yet the thought of unwrapping the gift
not yours, that small adultery.

    Does the gift unseen
remain the clarity of its symbol,
forever intended and pure?

Or does it become the bin
of all our dissatisfactions,
the public service writing
our analogies?

    There could, of course, be a movie based on this
but we would always forget its name

Just as right now, another
pulls on my sweater
thinking: the blind knit
    your golden thread

E)

                    for Rob

And do you remember that time
hiking to the abandoned trestle
Anthony your friend the weight-lifter
making all the noise the forest did not?
Even here as I write this, I can see
his great chest woofing the air
like he could drown in all of that.

And then
        down to the pot-holes
filled with spring water like bellies
of reclined nudes
the rock crisp and red
as our reflections walked
over the pools.

And do you remember the car ride back,
he talking of the atom bomb like a brother
and we'll do it again
                    we can do it again
his hands grabbing at something
invisible, his face red, burned
by inexplicable heat?

Do you remember the sound
of the air so deep
in his lungs?

But I wanted to ask you
not about Anthony
I just wanted to know—
do you remember
the cool of that water
the red sand on our feet?

5

Garden Time

thymus vulgaris

thymus vulgaris: the garden thyme used in cooking is a more shrubby
plant and came to Britain from the Mediterranean,
no doubt brought by the Romans.

All About Herbs

1

(economics of the garden)

garden time stretches like a tight ligament
from plants that look like weeds to
weeds that look like plants   (brought
by the romans no doubt). I've
removed half the carrots already
and have decided to dedicate this garden to
the free market. I will become *laissez-faire*
and leave the hoeing to the invisible hand.
I promise no interference. My garden
will weed itself.

2

lycopersicon esculenium

Your body is ripe
and red with what you
sentence to the compost
every month, a bit of you
articled to the second-hand
roots of the tomatoes and
their red rags of rain
and chicken-shit transfusions,
for these we have tended
and seeded
your long barren summer,
now we eat
and stain our lips
on borrowed blood.

(Enjoy! It's for you
I have picked
this basket of tongues!

3

raphanus sativus

Nobody loves a radish.

Some will fake a passing fancy or even insist
a burning lust but the radish
is always left to seed itself.

Taste the heartache between your teeth.

I dedicate this radish to all those
radishes.

4
salvia officinalis

Where gardening leaves off
sage takes you gently by the nose
and whispers: I know   I know.
Like the beginning to some greek tragedy
we know we have been here before
but we need to burn our tongues on sage again
prove the old gods have lost
none of their potency.

Sage shakes off the dust of delphi
and invites you to the shadows of the herb patch,
promising, with a sapient smile:

> you can still taste olympus
> you can still feel the wrinkled skin of a god

5

cochlearia armoracia: *Horseradish will swamp and kill off its*
near neighbours . . . it should be planted in
as isolated a place as possible, or not at all.

All About Herbs

(Stakeout)

A plant too hidden to be trusted
too insidious to be liked, even
its name sounds slightly psychotic.

> *Dear Ann,*
>   *My horseradish hides dynamite at night*
>   *makes prank calls to the peppers*
>   *brushes roots with the onions*
>   *picks on the peas*
>   *the corn pays just to stay alive.*
>   *Distraught in Donalda*

You see, horseradish regrets nothing.
It will burn the stomach that loves it, choke
the ground that grew it.
our favourite
sociopath of the garden.

> "The first kinde of Time is so well knowne
> that it needeth no description . . . I meane our
> common garden Time."
>
> John Gerard, The Herbal (1633)

6

amelanchier canadensis

(kind of blue)

The saskatoon reminds you that your love
should be as subdued as possible
and this little rampage through the berry patch
is what we all dream of—the perfect lover
who slips from his skin to stain our hands
with his dark purple kiss.

Yet it's all too perfect:

    sweeter than nipples
    sassier than rhubarb
    brassier than a solo sax

But this just shows
we can't make the rules.

                The saskatoon has always played
                the low down berry blues.

7
allium sativum

Those who love garlic know who they are
and know it's only a matter of time.

Garlic comes to us, wrapped
in parchment, holding
this little yellow sign:

The End Is Near
eat more garlic

> "How could such sweet and wholesome hours
> Be reckoned but with herbs and flow'rs?"
>
> Andrew Marvell, "The Garden"

8

cucumis sativus

Winter sleeps, cucullate,
in the cucumber patch
and its flurry of green.

Slice through their skin and
welcome to the ice age.

This is where frost hangs out
dreaming of glaciers,
where hail
seeds.

Yet every gardener knows
the cucumber betrays us.
Summer long they drift through the corn
like a nervous system,
all the while conspiring
with the freezer and the Frigidaire.

Don't let them fool you,
they are in league with December
and dance naked
at forecasts of snow.

Listen—

The cucumbers hum
through the night.

9
beta vulgaris

> "The great and beautiful Beet"
> Gerard

The beet sucks dirt,
keeping time.
If quarter notes grew,
they would grow with the beet,
the garden's rhythm and bruise.

If you've ever been
too good too lonely too bad,
put your ear to this heart;
if you've ever been too far gone
or not far enough,
wrap your lips around this
gentlest of wounds
let it bleed through your tongue
and when it says
just let it be
just let it be.

10
ribes grossularia

The gooseberry should have been my first lover.
We'd court each other
like nervous attorneys
whispering Latinate phrases
or maybe more in the way a typist
seduces the letter q *let's not be shy*
but, baby, let's not be quick.
The gooseberry taunts me
behind a moated grange of pricks.

> Of course it hurt
> we were both embarrassed
> but we both grinned.

A taste composed entirely
of early mornings and broken glass
with a hint of handcuffs and something
knotty, it tries to kill you a little,
but then the tongue desires death
to cup its cold *tabula rasa.*
Yet, before it wipes you out,
think of your first lover, the gooseberry,
and this white explosion:

The Garden

Winter has played with me
too much this year.
I bought the seeds to feel
the bombs in my hand.

Did I tell you that your potted fern had dried to origami on my
shelf?

> The home garden:
> My father refused its existence for 3 years,
> saying he couldn't understand the economics
> of land that small.
> My mother won through sheer patience
> and squatter's rights.
>
> Red potatoes green beans
> yellow beans peas corn
> and in one corner she let the thistle grow,
> told everyone they were the only flowers
> my father had ever brought her.
>
> He got so mad at her once
> he took out half the garden
> with one swipe of the 60-foot harrows.
> The only peas we ate that year
> were bought from the Hutterites
> and hardened by frost.
>
> To this day my father swears he won the argument.

I run the seeds through my fingers.

At the door, I see my mother,
hoe in her hand.

The garden is growing.

6

The Unified Field

I

Your letter a paper ball on the table beside me. I write you this reply.
Christmas had come and gone   snow piled in the eaves.
I remember, at times, a house full of laughing
and crying—both watering the same place.
Through the window, black poplar trees
and a landscape so empty it stuns the nerves.   *And what made you,*
my brother asked, *tell her in the first place.* Necessity,
I wanted to whisper, as if it really were
a matter of life.

II

Writing you this reply. You telephone to say
you will hang the bird house
I gave you for Christmas
from the wood shed.

        —Necessity, yes, basic as hunger
to be open for once.
For what are we if we must cushion our lives
with suitable fictions   If we must
close our doors to the swirling white
These are not questions
but resolve pushed too far.

                              If despair in this century
has become canonized   If law is measured
by the scars it inflicts   If a leaf cannot travel
from branch to ground—spiralling, earth-
                              skin—
without our noticing it
              and governing it—
                        When did the act of hanging
a bird house become simpler
than his touch?

III

I write this reply. Already the phrase
brings me comfort—a reply—
it is being written. Somewhere,
someone pushes blackness onto the whiteness of a page.
When something is unreliable you leave it, kill it
or coat it in art.
When the answers to our questions
are not what we expected
the air between us sizzles
we discover new ground.
                        The edge
of words is molten.
                        What else
if not life?

IV

And so it is written:
                    the same grain elevators
corrugated rust   oil lease roads thread
through black poplars to invisible darkness
fallen barns, russets and browns   the lake
the valley wall   the reptilian smell of old dirt.
Everything the same as it was last year   thick with recognition
and lack of human presence.   I think of your walks now—
a black speck on a page of white
moving through this snowscape.
                                        Trying to lose
all that is changing
                            Trying to lose
        all that can reply.

V

And is it so much now   for me
to say *I love him*   *He*
loves me

You say *No matter how far we advance*   *Regardless of how*
much the world will change   *There are ways*
that will never be accepted.

                    But a life in fiction will never protect us.

But we shed all this   and start over
start over with a few simple things?
Put on our woolen socks   sweaters
tie our boots and cotton scarves   Open the door
Open the door into this wheeling white   Open
this door
                    and walk?

VI

But since when has living in fiction been new?
Married to a drunk who died on you   Raised two kids
Cleaned office buildings for a living.
How often did this world need less telling   small diversions
small embellishments? Or maybe
it's the desire to peel back the flesh,
down   downto this single wire:
        the open door   the

                                    snow

VII

You say *In another century they would have hanged you
and everyone like you.*   Then there must be reasons
why this century has let me live.
Why I will not be beaten by someone's fists.
Why a lynching would not kill me.   Why even you
will not stop this reply. .   This is not heroism.
This is flesh *continuing*.

But try to believe these things do not happen
in this century   this year   in this very hour
and the fictions are starting again:
                        A man tied to a barbed wire fence
stripped and beaten   skull caved in by a pistol butt
                                    body doused in gasoline
    lit   left to burn
                        snow melting around him
        in luminous pools

                        outside our window   now
    in this century.

                            What, if not life?

        Fictions, more real than this?

VIII

Writing you this reply. Writing a defence
that should never have to be written.

IX

wolf willow   poplar   diamond willow
dogwood   blue spruce   saskatoon
they direct us over this landscape
puncture our walk with recognition. The cold
would finish you in hours if you stopped moving.
Survival, then, has taught us something of motion,
when the mind stumbles, we turn to the feet.
                                                    I follow
your trail from the window   You
a black spot a mile away   a single kernel   in all this
that would as soon forget you   wipe your footsteps
from its cerebral sleep.
How this land has shaped us, then,
where the strength comes from :   When even a walk
a clearing of the head   entails a fight   When even a breath
must be bargained for

short growing season is no explanation—

X

and we start our poems by writing of trees

XI

Writing you this reply I am
writing myself into clarity.

After twenty-five years what has changed between us:
instead of child and mother we are now adult

and adult, two who no longer understand
the landscapes over which the other has ridden.

And maybe this is right,
maybe every relationship should be laced

with an atom of hate
to give it structure—so we always know

from where we have come.
And we walk away

from our problems by walking
into them.

XII

My mouth over his chest   his skin
drifted beneath me   it has been a late night
and now the early morning   retinal black sky turns
iris blue   to give up all expectation   to give up
all motion   and not be pulled back into the moment
we mean only ourselves   we
exist   there is no philosophy stronger than this   sexual density
and if this is seen as unnatural by others
then, love,   we will be the most unnatural
we will be their match   their wood
            their fire

XIII

But to stop /
midway

To stop midway and think   the sound of snow under your feet
          barbed wire fence

                              empty

                                        singing

To look up through the poplar trees   each limb a horizon
a certainty
            sun low to your right   sun dogs
circling

To look up as your breath cracks through the air before you
                                        a molten expectancy
                        your hand in your pocket
grips the letter you will write   the conviction of your grasp
            each atom solid against skin

To sit at the kitchen table and watch you
stopped

XIV

midway   magpie off to the right
                                  filling the air with its hunger

To slow down   to stop   to look up myself
                          the fluorescent kitchen light crashing into me

To find significance in   the movement
            of thought through woods   the meditative
                                                    stopping
                          barbed wire fence
            to which no one is tied
                                        magpie now on the ground
                          pecks at something frozen
                                        its white becomes snow

How each beginning is filled with destruction   we walk
                          in opposition   and stop
in the woods
                to be killed
                                        to die
                or to think ourselves through

To hold a pen and know I will follow it
                through probability
                                through enmity
                                                stepping
across   this   page

XV

Where the edges blur
is where our interactions prove us

as we momentarily become part of the other
and we accept the difference

as our own: mother   son   His hand
on my *chest*   **There**   proves us

each probing the edges
tapping blind from room to room   Through

the glass now, I see you returning
your tracks behind you   thaw into white

poplars in the distance—probabilities
we must pass over in silence   The letter you will write—

the one your hand curls around—
the only piece of matter

still obeying all the rules.

XVI

Writing you this reply:
how new paths are created   laying them down
in repetition   until mistaken for nature
they become nature   These fights are old
but not useless

When our life is laid out for us   and our thoughts
do not vary outside its edges   When the rules are unbreakable
for nobody breaks them   When it is written
who and how you should touch

the snow falls outside our windows   each flake
a soundless tomb

Love will show us new landscapes
                              traced by the dark just rising
and we will follow behind
                                        in its wreckage
with our surveys and tools

XVII

You come in now   and bring completion with you
Your boots caked with snow   scarf frozen
each accessory another grid point we can depend on
We have spent how long today building
these separate silences   the ones we carry
bottled in words

                              When I say I want truth
I don't mean as a plane we momentarily pass through
but as a new space   with new rules   When I say life
I mean the time after

                         The moon splinters through the window
            The sound of trees cracking as the heartwoods freeze.

            These letters around me
                        the blank margins
                                    holding us
together
            in testament
                        in speech.

SHANE RHODES grew up in a small farming town in Central Alberta. He received his BA in English at the University of Calgary and his MA in English at the University of New Brunswick. He has published poetry, essays, reviews and articles in magazines, journals, and newspapers across Canada. He has also been an editor with filling Station, The Fiddlehead, and Qwerty. The Wireless Room, winner of the 1998 Alfred G. Bailey Award for Best Unpublished Poetry Manuscript from the Writers Federation of New Brunswick, is his first book of poetry. Shane lives in Calgary.